worn thresholds

JULIE BERRY

worn thresholds

Brick Books

CANADIAN CATALOGUING IN PUBLICATION DATA

Berry, Julie
  Worn thresholds

Poems.
ISBN 0-919626-75-0

1. Title.

PS8553.E77W6 1995   C811'.54   C95-930892-X
PR9199.3.B47W6 1995

The support of the Canada Council and the Ontario Arts
Council is gratefully acknowledged. The support of the
Government of Ontario through the Ministry of Culture,
Tourism and Recreation is also gratefully acknowledged.

Cover is after a photograph by Jan Row.
Author photo by Jan Row.

Typeset in Trump Mediaeval.
Printed and bound by The Coach House Printing Co.
The stock is acid-free Zephyr Antique laid.

Brick Books
431 Boler Road, Box 20081
London, Ontario
N6K 4G6

www.brickbooks.ca

acknowledgements

a few of these poems appeared in *Room of One's Own*, *Canadian Author and Bookman*, *Tabula Rasa*, *League of Canadian Poets Anthologies '91* and *'92*, *St. Thomas Chronicles*, *People's Poetry Letter*, and the University of Western Ontario's *applecore*.

thanks to janis rapoport and ted plantos, poets in residence at the st. thomas public library for their encouragement and to the roundhouse poets: john atkin, harry rudolfs, jan row, boh kinczyk, mike wilson and denise hay for their friendship and support through the years when these poems were being lived and written, and to marnie parsons and sheila deane for their editorial assistance.

contents

like other heavy things

year without rain

for lars, joel, james and thomas
and in memory of iva carmichael

jones's pond

jones's pond

the summer we were twelve
lorraine jones
deer-faced
chipped from born-again clay
led me up the back stairs
on rainy afternoons
to read harlequin romances
once she showed me
her parents' bedroom
recited their ritual
beds scraping
born-again groaning
it makes me sick   she said

evenings we walked on down
to jones's pond
past the red fox
pacing at the end of his dusty chain
past the poisoned corn
dead crows
baited traps
down on down to jones's pond
at the bottom of the
wet black forest
it just makes me sick   she said
and we slipped in
thin-legged girls
to swim

quiet as walls

1 sisters going nowhere in particular

swish tipped
of grass waist
deep green
for taste and hearing

dry of wave
wind for
brush against
young and skin

eleven as twelve as
whole as whole
suns blue or locked up
they don't care

ready for the fall
sisters
dreaming legs
gold furzed

of sumac limbs
groundhog below
still under rustle
for lonely

2 family waking

anything looms
fingering light and gray
doves of sorry
mourning who

earth turns a
white cheek drifts
west and cold
singing

leave taking the
by father secret razor
for sharp and keys
for shiny for jingle

four little girls
rise warm
breathing rafters
near and sweet

queen of shovels
pills aligned
be little
be white

3 queen of shovels

after music lotions
the pink sponge
bath look outside
eyes

o the enchanted
the smoothest flesh
and fish swim
up to look

mother's friend with
telescopes to see
strangers blowing far
candles out

towels and touch
the shrill undertow
lights mother's cigarette
it's she thinks him

he tickles littlest sister
red hair o shining
o running away
laughing and laughing

4 quiet as walls

of beds full
and beer too
many covers
big sister wakes up

he her cool
fingers he breathing
under hot
under covers

& face
shut & burning red
window up there
door over there

o not
o not
he makes
he her

when she tells
blank mother father
stare the bricks everything
quiet as walls

5 hail storm

on mother's hand
the promise or else
black seeds to
bury from want

riding through summer
roads gravel sharp
& mad &
dog panic

sky-ice of
broke over daughter
scrawny air hot
for blue petals

stems
bent shiny over over
wet and
drowned

for happy for
dance in dreams
in life too
delphiniums die

6 arrangement

snake grass advises in its unchanging tongue
she crawls tangled into trees
the highest branches sway
and the green miles hold her
the house is a roof
the gravel a road
people are very little and she
smallest of all

the mad red night prowls inside
but green ocean for
bare feet for
whispery wet
running up the sandy lane
the sun even
comes in
grandpa climbs the gas house roof
tin can tractor idling
fills her basket with wilder grapes
and grandma's painted desert comes when called
any morning she wants in their safe bed
nothing really wrong

hawks open the sky over dying fields
waiting for earth to turn enough
bring them home to winter breathe she can she
lets them in and they bring her more cold blue
space than she needs enough to let her
breathe and love to the cold cold core

childhood of the medical missionary

her first house filled with black smoke
a bat lived in the stairwell of the second
in mount hope hurricane hazel
slapped goldfish big as pop bottles
against the attic windows
and in fingal zorro and daddy came home
the same time every friday

the big arm chair forever swallowing her
in one house   coughing her up in another

she learned fast
daddy's magazines
all the eyes blacked out
the messy hallways   edge-of-town murder scenes
co-eds raped and strangled
mothers beaten and shot
the whereabouts of the panties always so important

the night soldiers
dragged their seeing-eye boots into the basement
stomped on the thin necks of her little sisters
but she escaped   crouched behind the summer clothes boxes
memorizing gray's anatomy
the chinese alphabet
and all the books of the new testament

paradise

i found paradise at glen manderson's backyard circus
a penny for this
a penny for that
but paradise was a nickel

i wanted to see
how they'd fit it in a moldy tent
paid my nickel and lifted the flap
in the dark i saw a dish on a tv table
in the dish a pair of dice

paradise i whispered syllable by syllable
all the way down elmhurst
to brookmere
& home

where the babies come out

when we were seven patty pekeski and i had a bath together
what's that she asked pointing to the light brown line
that divided my abdomen in half
that's where the babies come out i told her
when the baby gets too big the skin splits along there
with my finger i followed the line from my belly button down
what about all the blood she asked
it's kind of like when god parted the red sea i told her
he makes sure you don't bleed much

uncle jim

uncle jim wearing his apron in the back kitchen on hughes street
baking cherry pies
there's the scratch the stretcher made
carrying him out
jane and susan and julie
hopscotch and bee stings
driveway cinders
when it rained they took turns
being cinderella on the porch

he died in the kitchen
flour on his fingers
pie in the oven
there's the scratch the stretcher made
carrying him out
while jane and susan and julie
made tea in the gully
under winter vines
tea with twigs
and bits of black ash floating

convertibles to hardtops

my father's first convertible
was orange and grey
orange like tomato soup
the campbell soup car we called it
a used '58 dodge convertible
my little sisters and me
sitting across the back seat
net scarves on our heads
plastic sunglasses
grimacing into the wind all the way up kipling avenue
north into the caledon hills

his second convertible was brand new
a white '62 thunderbird with red upholstery
we can't afford this my mother said
dad would drive the car across the road to mainprize drugstore
park it by the curb with us girls in the back
net scarves tied around our necks
sunglasses in place
he'd go in for cigarettes or comics or gum
i'd see him wait behind the glass for somebody to stop and
admire the car
then he'd breeze out
jump into the driver's seat
hang on girls he'd say zooming away
and up into our driveway across the road

when my father got fed up with family life
he'd say we were lucky he didn't up and buy a harley
and head off into the wild blue
and he meant it
i remember thinking that was generous of him
to leave us his convertible
after the thunderbird came the red '63 dodge
and then the '65 honey-gold chev

the summer i was sixteen
my father taught me to drive
in his last convertible
a yellow '67 ford ltd
driving home alone east of rondeau
top down and no seat belt
my wheels slipped off the pavement into loose gravel
i jerked the wheel and the car spun
slow golden circles
i remember how my words like ballast
maintained their weight and order
this   is   an   accident
i   am   having   an   accident
while the cornfields melted into green soup

nobody coming either way
and when i stopped spinning
i was in the ditch right-way-up
both hands on the steering wheel
i figured i'd died and slipped into another world
leaving my remains smeared all over highway 3
i figured this new world'd be different
pulled out of the ditch
and drove home
but nothing changed except my father switched from
convertibles to hardtops

what i want to know is how many dimensions exist on this world
and if there are infinite numbers can one be exactly the same as
another except one man chooses to buy hardtops instead of
convertibles and in the dimension before i spun out on highway 3

would the man who bought convertibles decide to stay with his wife and not fool around with the lady half his age who drove a black corvette because maybe just maybe the convertibles struck the perfect balance for him or could it be that the man in the other world who decided after his daughter spun out on highway 3 to switch to hardtops was finally so bored by all those hardtops that he could not resist the lady in the black corvette

poor man's pine

grandma's rinsing warm blackberries
adding sugar
it's hotter'n the hubs of hell
something in grandpa's voice pounds the dark under the back
    porch
the beds upstairs are dreaming painted deserts
and the world raining and raining
when the needle sticks
hotter than   hotter than   hotter than

you can lead a woman to blackberries says grandpa
but you can't make her pick or blueberries neither
ugly enough to eat hay says grandpa
ugly enough
the kettle boils
grandma asks who
grandpa's on to aunt ellen's falsies
grandma's tight sweaters
slop bucket needs dumpin dad
grandpa hauls himself out of his chrome and plastic chair
six flies follow him out the door

land's so por a rabbit'd hafta pack a lunch to cross it
paul who died so young would have loved that
as much as the oriole's nest by the railroad trestle over sunset
floating as he does between the line of norway spruce
and the falling down tobacco kiln
and me in the red corduroy dress that jim admired so
dancing backwards across fields choked with poor man's pine

worn thresholds

letters to mary anne

after 23 days at sea
birds with the faces of dead sailors fall at my feet
i send them to you mary anne
a crossbill and a snowbird
a triton rears its frightful head
loops its tail across the horizon
they say i'm fond of map drawing
they say i'm fond of gaiety
i'd rather sail to corvo than go down to tunbridge wells
the scheme would be more enlarged
the compass never works
i swear mary anne no one ever knows where we are
rats snipe and so forth
the dinner oversets
how we laugh when the tea things break
even so i eat broth without spilling

the end of july at fort erie and hot
i sleep in a dirty house these nights
and with no one to drive
go nowhere
the afternoon i set out with francis
to drive myself to mrs tice's
the sky is dark and heavy
everywhere green
so much green it makes me cold
i crave brown
it would take only a little to warm me
but there is none so i wear two fur tippets
the road is very bad and francis cries
i'm afraid he might bounce out
so i stop and tie him to the seat
when we get to mrs tice's we have tea
did i mention the pigeons mary anne

how they darken the sky
and drink the pond dry
how the men stand on the roof
and pluck them from the sky
we eat their wings and breasts salted
from a barrel
sixty years later the butler
pushes me in my chair across the wet grass
each morning until i die
the parish priest
delivers my eulogy one long afternoon
but mary anne
all they've kept is my presentation skirt
you remember the flowered brocade
it's on a pedestal now
in the hall

letters to elizabeth

when your packet of letters arrives
eliza kisses the margins of every page
your fingers have touched here
and here and here she says but i
cross the room
mi mas querida Amiga
if you'd died i could not miss you more

rain and snow keep us indoors now
eliza pale as fields reads spanish to us most afternoons
she's learned the sky by heart and wants a deeper book
your aunt says i mustn't teach your girls anything
until they're 12 or 15
but i pay no attention
eliza's grammar is impressive
and charlotte's taking well to french
caroline's full of odd fancies
harriet's memorized your letters
and recites them at dinner
eliza says she would gladly give two frocks
a petticoat and her green sash in exchange for wings
so she could fly to you

the girls came to dinner again
we drank a toast to your health
and eliza cried a bit
that's just the same as we do she said

it's been two years since you left
your aunt is buying silver plates by the dozen
and the axminster carpet from walford
has been cut down to fit the back room
harriet has drawn a very good ear and
i enclose it
the other drawings are stained badly
though they were washed twice in milk
what do you think of my sonnet to a goldfinch

when i get to hembury fort your vigil in the canvas house
will drive me out of doors
and i too will read german and don antonio de guevera
all night imagining you here

james had my death hole in germany published anonymously
and called it cavern of death
as a result i have received twenty pounds
and a proposal of marriage
i told my suitor i intend to continue single all my life
a fortnight later he gave me a moth
a brown furry thing
but i let it go out the window after he was gone
have you heard ladies about to be married now present their
husbands with drawings of their limbs
most often an arm but lady susan gordon gave the duke of
manchester one of her legs

it's no use
nothing i have compares to your tomahawk
and the possibility you may have to eat the dog
here the poor are restless
corn's high and there are riots at honiton
i bought a fish at billingsgate
but there will be no oranges until april
i'll send the marmalade with captain lowe in may

where are you now elizabeth
i unfold your rivers across my bed
your forests and rutted roads
tell me there's a field near you
where i might build myself a shed
your aunt says i ought not be your friend
she fears i'll consult you about my lovers
that's easily overcome i tell her
i'll have no lovers

tongue prints

my heart's gritty after all these miles
even with the windows up
dust gets in
better to roll them down
lean out
eat it all up

just ask
i'll lick the dust off your bumper
leave little tongue prints
up the trunk
the back window
over the roof
down the windshield
face-first over the front bumper

you can run over me
for all i care
run over me in your warm dusty car

word in your mouth

i want to be the word in your mouth
the word you love best
i want to float
rising and sinking in the air
that stirs with every page you turn
i want into that gasp
when the line you need
comes for you
better than you'd imagined

spill me all over your page
let me soak through
til your ink runs

o your writing
the firm thrusts
of your downstrokes
the lightened ease
of your up

in the dark

love of words has brought her here
she takes his hand
presses it over her mouth
his other over her eyes
straining to speak   to see
her words
become more perfect
when squeezed out
from between his fingers
her sight more pure
in the dark
beneath his hand

eclipse

the usual moon
at its brightest and roundest
is flat and out of reach
but i could hold this bruised plum
this

    moon

the 6th day you're gone

i'd rather love on earth

consider for a moment neptune's moons
all eight
there's triton with its purple stains
and nereid
the others all unnamed
earth's single moon works best
lovers parted need not agree
which moon is which

try standing on neptune
you'll sink
there is no solid ground
only volcanoes
that once flowed liquid ice
imagine a world that cold and no place to stand

last night before snow

the path to this place is harder than earth should be
like the entrance to a building
meant to last
but by the river it
softens
sinking
joe pye weed
cattails   purple vetch
queen anne's lace
rising up all round

the lovers take this place
hold it closer than skin
eat it up before they go away
later watch it grow
up through the cracks of sidewalks
it appears in rooms full of people
they shake their heads
to clear the air of drifting pollen
but it settles on everything
and they hold very still
this is the part they love

flowers change
by august it's touch-me-nots
goldenrod   asters
and pearly everlasting
the last night before snow
the lovers lie under layers of poems
crow song
river song
they listen
measure the future
with each leaf
as it falls
through its
private
dark

worn thresholds

fat and responsive
as a cow's tongue
my need drags me across
this salt lick love
this hollow you save for me
comforting as the worn thresholds
of significant old buildings

the only thing my father taught me

spring comes grimacing
through slits of melting snow
we take careful steps
dogwood sings
its new fire confused
by our hiss and sizzle
ironwood trees
the only thing my father taught me
i teach you
strongest in the forest when alive
quickest to rot when dead
why waste time you say and follow at a safe distance

years from now in late fall
driving down back concessions
i'll see the crows
revise every fence row
i'll watch the vulture
that holiest of birds
waiting beside the patient ditch
faith will keep the road from straying off
and my face in the rear-view mirror
will be a page
its corner turned down
to save a place

so many more crazy people

there's a psychiatric hospital at the edge of town
that used to be an armed forces training base but after the war
there were so many more crazy people than soldiers
they turned it back into a psychiatric hospital

i worked there the summer i was nineteen
and i still remember margaret and emily
mavis mrs sharpe stella
albert mrs polonanski
and barbara
she'd had a stroke while cutting rhubarb pies at a church supper
every morning she woke up in a strange place
who are you dear she would ask a hundred times a day
i'd tell her but she'd forget
where am i
in a hospital i'd say but by then she'd be asking
who are you dear
sometimes she'd ask for her husband bill
her daughters francie and sandra
did they get some more turkey
and while i explained about the hospital she'd look at me
who are you dear

when you're young the bodies of old people are like foreign
countries you never expect to visit
every morning i eased their gray sad bodies
into tubs of warm water
holding them by their first names
i learned to pry their fingers off my wrists gently
at first i refused to slam their imaginary doors
and squash their imaginary bugs
i got so i'd do it
just to get a few minutes of peace and quiet
pretending in that instant before the act
that i too could see the angels
the demons
the bugs with human faces

margaret's madhouse

demons hang from doorknobs
devils lurk in the dark of keyholes
bite the meat of her hand
doors have undone her
once she loved a man

touching him
her hands turned to
                wings
    feathered
white

having the baby was the worst
blood follows her now
down all the shining hallways

she begins by loving her hands

she finds them one morning
on a train between winnipeg and edmonton
folded in her lap
after a long night
over the blue star strip club
with a man from kitchener
whose name she forgets

she leaves them lying around sometimes
so she can come across them
by accident
so she can say   what nice hands
like she's seeing them for the first time

staying clean

there are women

who live their lives
standing up
doing what they cannot help
just out of sight
quick & quiet
often breathless seldom
caught

or they drop out of childhood
already rotting inside
out they leave their bare footprints
on the windshields on
the ceilings of cars
their purses on the dark beach
of every brief affair

or like ferrets
they swallow themselves
teeth-first down dark holes
for fathers   husbands   lovers
flush out the prize   then shine
like sunward mirrors
smooth & hard
a perfect surface
to reflect a world poised
somewhere between mischief and malevolence

but there are women who will not sneak
they climb their flimsy scaffolding
nailing themselves together as they go
some fall apart
or their hearts stop
a few will teeter
all their clumsy lives

dissection kit

when i was 19 i bought a dissection kit
all the instruments in their places
safely strapped down
the case was black leather
inside the red velvet was breathing
i took its pulse
careful not to touch the instruments
bits and pieces of my face were on them

the case is empty now
i threw it out
afraid to think
where all those instruments had gone
but a woman needs to know such things
a woman must keep house better than that

i don't remember which one went where
i swallowed several eagerly
some i misplaced during operations
i had to leave the room so often
to change diapers   wash dishes
rock babies to sleep
even if i turned the light off and shut the door
i had to leave the incision open
there was never enough time to finish
and when i came back
i would find someone else had been there
removed things without asking
sewn up the incision
another instrument missing

and the rest   i'm not sure
sometimes i'd catch my children
playing with them
and i would put them away
out of reach
but they'd always turn up
under the piano   behind the stove
or mixed in with the knives and forks
biding their time
growing arms
and legs

giving birth

i am julie
daughter of ruth
daughter of eulia
daughter of a woman from comber
who died giving birth

giving birth
as if having a baby has nothing
to do with pain or blood
as if having a baby is like going to a birthday party
giving a present
wrapped up pretty
handed from one pair of clean hands
to another
to be unwrapped
and admired

someone once told me
a woman shows her true character during childbirth
real ladies remain ladies as the babies come out
when i had my first baby i heard the woman down the hall
screaming obscenities
i kept my lips together when the nurses
put my heels into the steel stirrups
i was proud of my restraint as the pain increased
surpassed all expectation
the doctors danced and waved their tongs
good girl they said
i had three more babies after that one
and never raised my voice
not once

i am julie
daughter of ruth
daughter of eulia
daughter of a woman from comber
no one remembers her name

the sad truth about words

someone help the woman
who writes *em evol*
backwards on the window of her 17th story apartment
she has learned the sad truth about words

and the woman under today's headline
Murder By Partners a Silent Epidemic
hands cover her mouth
she's sickened by the fine print
certain of another swindle

we need a language without holes or grappling hooks
a language smooth and useful as a spoon
where a woman can stand
far from the sentences
lumbering like circus trains through inattentive towns
every word a locked cage
the chesapeake and ohio
cowcatcher and all

instruments of adjustment

she gave the bed to goodwill
two men took it away
in the back of a yellow truck
helping the handicapped help themselves
written on the side
it was a big bed
queen size
procrustes
stretched her on his rack
to make her fit
some days she found the bed too small
and she would find pieces of her body on the floor
procrustes trimmed her overhanging limbs
when required

near the end
the bed got so high
she couldn't see the floor
stepping out into the cold air of the bedroom
was a leap of desperation
though some would call it faith

now she sleeps alone
in a prettier bed of cherry
finely turned and carved
she is still intimate with the ceiling tiles
and the wallpaper grows more spirited as it fades
procrustes has gone away
sometimes she finds his cruel instruments of adjustment
in the pockets of old clothes
she touches them
with unaccountable pleasure

after the divorce

my children sleep upstairs
i sleep down
god knows what time it is
one cricket left in the garden
a big fly bumps and buzzes around my light
heads into a darker room
again i am visited by the limbless bride
seventeen years wearing the same pearly bodice
amazing how much a woman can get done without arms or legs
she always blames the groom for the tragedy
for reaching in and pulling everything out
he couldn't help it i tell her
you never locked your doors

looking back my footprints are full of melting snow
and ahead they are deep and
empty and far far apart

drain poem

my mother calls and we get on the topic of my divorce
discuss the what-went-wrong
move along to other things
a recipe for spaghetti sauce
the price of orange juice
suddenly my drain starts to gurgle
loudly   rhythmically
my mother hears it too

your drain is talking to you dear

yeah but i never listen

the drain churgles and chugs

it knows i'm listening dear
it's calling out to me

yes mother
my drain would know your voice anywhere

the drain clears its throat
there's a long wet silence

you know dear
your frank was death to drains

yes i know mother

even *my* drains plugged up
in that short time he stayed with me
that man would run anything down a drain

maybe that's what did it mom
the bathroom sink had been complaining for years
but it was finally the kitchen sink that broke down
it gagged for months before giving up
we tried everything
drano   liquid plumber
must've gone through a half dozen plungers

a kettle full of boiling water dear
every week or so
that's all it takes to keep
a drain clear

the drain hiccoughs hopefully
we say good-bye

i fill the kettle
turn the burner on high

pieces of sandra

pieces of sandra are surfacing in the harbour at kincardine
a registered nurse out swimming felt something brush against her
arm when she managed to grab hold of it and look at it she saw it
was a piece of human jaw with four teeth attached
revulsed by this discovery she threw the thing back into the
water and swam to shore
how does one comb a harbour yet it was combed

i look at my hands my arms legs
surprised to find everything's there
how can this be when parts of me so often drift away
like mosquitoes looking for that one essential meal

canoe trip

phil throws a fresh-caught pickerel onto the rock
fishes up three cans of beer and a bottle of white wine
from the bottom of the canoe
misplaced in the general drunkenness of the night before
the pickerel's round eye stares
his mouth opens and closes patiently
nothing has prepared him for this
soon the men are drunk
i've got a buzz on says phil
to the north a loon calls
and another from the south
in the stillness that follows hugh sighs
beautiful eh?
yeah says phil   i just had an orgasm
they laugh delightedly
phil crashes off through the trees to get his food pack
later while the fish fries on the pan the men talk fishing
a real fisherman never comes til he's called laughs phil
a fine presentation of the lure gives him a hard-on
a bit of a marshy edge says hugh

the next night on the shore of rocky island lake
mayflies dance with their reflections on the glass-calm surface
behind her the fire crackles
phil says it's too bad the women won't skinny dip
hugh agrees
in the morning the sun
burns the tops off the pines across the lake
we set out for the portage into sanguish
when the wind comes up strong in the afternoon
we decide to camp at a deserted hunting lodge
two cabins with tin roofs
doors missing
in a tin boat long abandoned on shore i'm reading denise levertov
        insofar as poetry has a social function it is to awaken
        sleepers by other means than shock if you commit yourself
        to poetry you will not drift through your years half awake

the next night we camp on a rock
it takes 14 rocks to hold our tent down
i hold the aluminium poles
while the storm rumbles away to the east
i realize i am deathly sick of the quietness of people
i know a man who once hired a bunch of carpenters just to get rid
of a squeaky floorboard
his wife hired the same crew to get the squeaks back

she contemplates enjambement

while carrying plastic laundry baskets
up and down stairs
in the cellar she sorts the dirty clothes
neo-classic   baroque   rococo
and slaps her naughty children
in iambic pentameter
she seeks the ever-concealed
never-revealed
source of all dirt
while truth simmers
in the kitchen
and stacks of half-written poems
gather dust
in the cool basement of her brain

to be a mother

is to re-route chaos
is to channel disaster
is to corner the little buggers
and kiss them all over

bulldozed by a fat-cheeked boy

when she wakes up the furniture is becalmed the heavy-legged
table longs for the dance to begin and the four-poster bed's been
considering suicide so long so long she rails since i've done a
pirouette in her dream she follows a man carrying bed rails over
his shoulder like fishing poles or guns under the peach trees
they find a china cabinet finally he's got what he wants
a small glass animal and he holds it up to the light turning it
different ways anyway it's all gone now the tiger lilies too and
the wild grapes bulldozed by a fat-cheeked boy whose father rents
the land

suicide note for isis

above your wheat sheaf crown
entwined with serpents
in the air beside your gown
letters float
e clings to your breast
moments from your tongue
delicious
and i so hungry these thirty years

learned daddy's alphabet at two
what else could i do
but make a monkey bar poem
a monkey bar jail
with my tin pail
my rattle wired with mommy's bones
words clanged down

prizes only made me sadder
but the bonfire saddest of all
and i just
have to
dear sweet frieda goodbye goodbye
my darling baby nicholas

tape and wet towels
two glasses of milk
slices of bread and butter
blankets
open windows

now in the freezing hallway
my blue fist holds the postage
for tomorrow's cancellations
you shake your hair
shower seeds
a new alphabet sprouts quiet
and polite
no shouting or crying out
let us
may we
pray allow us to ...

i open my mouth and eat them

i climb the stairs

my face lies safe on the oven rack
babies warm in their windy room
notes mailed
one pinned to the pram

my lover's ex-neck and why

and why the hairdresser's giant purple nails
with square ends

why the soft
skin of my lover's ex-neck

and another thing
why the smoothness of the skin of my lover's ex-neck and the
squared-off ends of the hairdresser's giant purple finger-
nails and the trophies
the huge trophies in the in the huge
trophies in the shining in
the window

and why the purple nails the big purple nails
of the hairdresser

because the soft skin of my lover's ex-neck in his ex-car
because his wife rubs the feet of their palsied son and makes
aardvarks out of paper and water and glue

because my friend moans at the typewriter and tells stories
of two women who live together because she types with two
fingers and moans and says this is not and sighs working right
and the plastic virgin kneels on earl's chair hands folded
and because of water striders and raccoons and the curling
tendrils of my lover's ex-hair as it lies against his damp ex-
neck where i long to press my ex-lips remembering the moon and
the fire-pits when lake erie simmered and the world was smaller
than any word we settled on

staying clean

you have nice eyes says ron
eyes are strange organs she says
all that aqueous solution
last month ron sat on his deck
every afternoon
in suburban saskatoon
and watched his neighbour charlie
dig a four foot deep trench
around the house
once when charlie stopped
he saw ron watching him
have you checked your eaves
he shouted over the hedge
what are eaves asked ron

what if we didn't see the world
through these turgid balls of salty water
she asks herself while ron busies himself
under her dress
light molecules vibrate faithfully
over his shoulder
transferring the tv
the shrubbery outside the window
into her
eyes are a buffer zone she decides
shifting her hips slightly
as important as the distance
from here to saskatoon

without these buffer zones she thinks
the world would burn indelible
images on our retinas
everything we see would remain before our eyes
even when we turn away
she pictures that blurr
shuts her eyes throws back her head and moans
she calculates how soon you would go blind
breathing hard and fast she thanks her lucky stars
for distance
for buffer zones
for the way a woman can stay clean
not touching her life
even as it pins her down

like other heavy things

a way of seeing

i have a friend who makes me look at things
up close
rocks   dirt   twigs
how they lie this way or that
not that i'm unobservant
i was never that

another friend points out angels
now i can't go out without staring up
and when the air curdles
begins to vibrate
i'm positive
a whole choir of angels is about to show up

i don't want perfection
or a state of continual bliss
i've heard they begin to smell
the moment they arrive
it's depth i want
to see the backs of things without
losing sight of their fronts
that gap between intention and effect
that space
the reason we go on trying
the reason we don't

like other heavy things

solemn vows
like other heavy things
pianos   boulders
have been known to suddenly rise
float over our heads
speed purposefully to more suitable locations
in dreams this unpredictability of what matters
is natural as clouds
but if you are awake when your piano rises
crashes through the front window and floats away
over the neighbour's blue spruce
you are startled
you question your sanity
you are out one piano

cemetery tour

we are waiting for mr peters the mayor to start the tour
he does local history when he's not loading groceries
into cars at the a&p or being mayor four blocks west
it's getting late so mr cosens starts us off
my first cemetery tour
though cemeteries have always been my thing
i never took my kids to parks for picnics
always graveyards
the old ones are best
you can always find an old tombstone fallen over
the egg salad sandwiches   cookies   apples
spread out over the rest in peaces
the borns the dieds the beloved wifes of

mr leroy garbet wearing blue pants
holds his mouth like he's chewing the end of a weed but he's not
passes by saying to nobody
can't find my grandmother anywhere
married three times and nobody remembers
what name she's buried under
he wanders off chewing on his imaginary weed while mr cosens
tells us the facts
who contributed what
mr southwick and mr penwarden and mr farley
mr reek the grocer
mr husik the butcher
mr williams gave $5000 for the old folks home
james hutchison was killed at the battle of fish creek
mr barbridge who owned the star theatre and ran a shoe store
drove off the wilson ave bridge
some said he did it on purpose some said he was drunk

mr cosens mentions four women in the ninety minute tour
mamie chamberlain a kindergarten teacher
was distantly related to neville
the last duel in canada was fought over sarah hughes and the

winner got to marry her
helen turner was a lingerie clerk at anderson's for 40 years
alicia tutty fell asleep at leamore park

there are as many women as men under the ground
it's not mr cosens fault he doesn't talk about any of them
he doesn't know anything about them
nobody thought to keep track
wife of
wife of
beloved wife of

we're following mr cosens around the graveyard
when a big beige car pulls up
it's the mayor's mother come to tell us he won't be coming
something's come up
the st thomas ladies slow pitch association meeting
she rolls her eyes
you know steve
he loves graveyards
he'd be here if he could
he'd pick a cemetery any day over a baseball diamond

mr leroy garbet tells me
he dug the canna lily bulbs up
out of the city flower beds last week
they'd throw them out anyways he says
i got them in the basement   the bulbs
they'll grow this high
he reaches as high as he can
next year the leaves'll be the colour of
he looks around
the colour of
and he points off through the monuments
that bus shelter over there

famous poets must endure much

if i'm famous enough someday
maybe someone will preserve my brain
put it in a jar on a shelf
label it Poet/Female
famous poets must endure much
walt whitman for instance
his brain fell right off the plate
while scientists scrutinized it
after that unfortunate mishap
it was of no use to anyone

daisy cole's woods

in daisy cole's woods
jan points out the wilted leaves of wild leeks
pokes at trilliums with a stick
they're almost done she says
we look at the flowers
their solemn froth pink-turning
i think of the blown-up words
taped to my walls
hanging from windows
how the light shines through the stanzas
things i know fight for a place in my throat
thistles are edible when peeled
paintain's good for burns
burdock tea

at the edge
harrowed fields rise like waves
everywhere dirt is higher
than we are
we turn back into the woods
jan says be careful of your boots
be careful of your shoes
your books
your words
everything can be eaten she says
i step carefully through the maidenhair fern
or is it meadowrue i ask
who cares what it's called says jan
a hillside of young ashes swallows her legs
foxtail's good for scrubbing pots i advise
seconds before she disappears

season of granite

the wind delights
upon superior
continents of calm
oceans of ripple
my body rests on rock
but the season of granite
is nothing to me

i consider the butterfly's
brief island of flutter and glide
and if i want substance
i hold my three-year-old's hand
the memory of his fat jam-pot fingers
cool and sticky
in my mind

waiting for the 4 o'clock train

consider mrs wilson confined to her walker
waiting for the 4 o'clock train to windsor
rope off your body with bright
plastic police-caution ribbon
your search for the promised land
begins with a long wait

the first step to the promised land
a ghost step
like the one at the top
or bottom of a very dark stair
mrs wilson is suspended here
waiting for the train
the 4 o'clock train to windsor
the train that never comes
though she asks again and again
year after year
no one thinks to tell her
she has to get to the station first

so life works for most of us
the promised land like an itch
at the back of your tongue
explains so much
why mrs wilson waits
miles from the station
why you wonder
enough for any poem

canoeing (from the photograph)

in early morning we draw light
a great fan of ripples
behind us   a barge of
calm

when night comes we pull light in
strand by dripping strand
wind it on our fingers   fleshy spools
and pile it on the darkening shore

what miraculous spiders
these great white paws
pulling in and in and in
careless fistfuls
      come to us sweet light
we whisper
and weave a blistering
night-flower

help

the children are learning to yell for help
at the public swimming pool
help help   shout the little ones
that's not loud enough   say the instructors
HELLLLLP   they try again
better   say the instructors

no one comes to help them
i guess they're practising that too

more permanent holes

i remember joan and me in her kitchen
seeking relief from lonely motherhood
tea in china cups stirred with tiny spoons
our sons walking under the table
we would lay the spoons down
and pick them up and lay them down again
in that kitchen her husband
put the muzzle of a gun into his mouth
some holes disappear as soon as you make them
spoons are good for that
guns make more permanent holes

in my jake dream
susie his sister
turned him over
all the planet earth kept jake inside himself
til susie turned him over
and he gushed out the hole in his chest
straight up
like old faithful
bits of torn paper and twisted wreckage
you could hear it for miles

we want to know the meaning
of joan's husband and jake
we hope it will begin to make sense
it's what makes us crazy in the end

pipes

my sister says he always promised the first one asleep a quarter
i don't remember getting any quarters but now whenever i think a
hug is expected the air goes thick and my body doesn't want it
after what uncle sid did the pipes in his sooty house shuddered
and groaned whenever we turned on a tap after what uncle sid did
to me under the covers in the back bedroom in his sooty house
across from kellog's
and i don't remember any quarters

in the quiet room in the small quiet room where he made me
touch
touch him
in the quiet room under the covers
when he took my cool hand and made me hold his
his   thing
there was no sound
but his fat red breath
no sound
i could make
i couldn't say
in the small quiet room when uncle sid did that i
couldn't say   don't

years later at my cousin's wedding
my three sisters and i in the ladies room
sitting with our long dresses hitched up
in separate pink cubicles
looking at the things you look at in those places
your feet   the floor tiles
we told
and then we laughed
inventing words for what he did to us
because there were none that we knew
we came out   fixed our hair   our faces
we didn't speak of it again for twenty years

mostly i remember
the shuddering pipes in that house
and sometimes think our sadness
seeped into the plumbing
with every drink of water
every washing of our hands
where do the pipes of torn-down houses go
and what becomes of the shuddering

outside my window i hear light traffic
and a bird swallowing air
jewelled gulps of sound
falling down its throat

i don't get that joke he says

early saturday morning thomas
lying beside me asks
which way will we fall when gravity's done
i point at the ceiling
oh he says   i thought we'd fall into the world

i wonder about trees in a weightless world
how they'd stay rooted in earth
twigs and leaves pointing into outer space
imagine autumn that year
all the oxygen would go up
sand   placemats   anniversary clocks
everything

i've learned to take nothing for granted
gravity exists for now
my bed on the floor
straight planks
running up and down the rooms
thomas asks   which way will the people in china fall

suddenly i know
hardwood/abyss
mascara/abyss
french doors and wrenches
i whisper abyss
into my son's blind eye
i don't get that joke he says

wolf story

tutuyea made the caribou's eyes
sad and only a little afraid
she curled its foreleg around the wolf
it's almost tender
this caribou-wolf embrace

i make tutuyea dead for my poem
she carries her tongue on her back
shaped like a wolf
the story flows out
passes before tutuyea's closed eyes

holding the wolf story with both hands
she touches her lips to the polished stone
cool and smooth
it falls through her hands
and makes the world

year without rain

year without rain

last winter it never snowed
the ground froze hard and brown
spring was dry as dry
my blood went green
black-green
that black that red blood goes
you always forget i know i do

dreamed of two-headed turtles
legless frogs
bellies slack all the cold
blood tamped off green
hearts be damned &
everyone i loved left town or
died i didn't care

lips dried up
everything dusty and a line
of nothing down my spine split in
two nothing lines for two legs
& down to my down to my
heels & out like sun rays
in little kids' paintings

tongue raging
in & out in &
my eyes wouldn't
close my skin
was that tight
& clothes
hurt so i
went without

watching pale sky i
heard the rapid crackle of skin
rip behind me like water poured on ice
cubes my feet fell away i saw
them sad as old
shoes seconds before my
face hit the floor the
pieces crawled off
edges curling

dreamed of sleek-tailed rats
wingless sparrows when i woke
up i licked air thick as jelly
flicked in mouthfuls of smell i
wanted to get up my arms
what about my
arms i squirmed my
belly slid across the floor

the answer to your prayers

let's say you find out
early one spring
you've got cancer
your lover begins to miss his wife
your husband's sorrow
drags itself across every sky

let's say you pray for your life
to go on

accomodating
the machine turns on
off & on
the answer to your prayers
clicks and whirrs

the big machine
hangs like the last word
of a love affair
a holy punctuation mark

the technicians consult your chart
joke about the lead lollipop
as they slip it into your mouth
position the lead chunks above your face
then sidle into another room
to watch the grid
you're spread upon
this is radiation

the seconds

you know there are places
the sinister rays leak
or go bouncing off

the cement walls
ring with ricochetting light

your face is screwed
to the table

the seconds

there is finally a smell
the smell your hands pick up
from fondling keys
or other objects you'd rather not need

you hear the technicians coming back
talking in tongues
you feel them wince
where the green hallway turns

their scented fingers
remove the lead chunks
above your face
your drawn and quartered face
their lips move
talk about the heat
on their day off

as you lift your head
you think the strangeness
of heat
burning so politely
in this room
you sit up
turn your body
watch your sandals
touch the floor

your blessed toes
so safe
so far away

the wings themselves

she sits on the floor back to the wall hands folded on her
lap for hours our talk has entered the space in her guest
room and lighted on the old dresser the bed our heads and
shoulders our words the hollow-boned birds of summer no
longer frantic for food for babies or worried for fear they
won't fly but flying out for joy

she tells me of the day she sprouted angel wings how she
always knew she could fly and this knowledge she has given
me feels much heavier than the angel wings must feel and i
tell her or maybe only wish i had that i always knew she
could fly and i saw her wings rather felt them fanning me
the day she walked into my hospital room after they had
carved a piece out of my mouth

and were feeding me through a tube even so i could still
taste the bits of my flesh before i swallowed them and
now i want to apologize for bringing my flesh into this
so i will sorry but that's what makes the knowledge of
your wings so much heavier than the wings themselves

touching ground

started a story about how i lost my virginity and my velvet hair
ribbon on the beach at port bruce how i stayed up all night
looking for the ribbon

while my son has his tonsils out i wait in a room
furnished with a plastic bench a coke machine a tv and
this sign:

> a voice will come over
> the loudspeaker calling
> your name be prepared
> to answer in a strong
> voice you will then be
> given an important message

my nightmare woman's hair is too black
lips too red
she has no arms or legs
the beaded bodice of her wedding dress sparkles
she makes love to the least human
creature in the room
convince me i am loved
convince me
convince me
the ones with eyes watch
she smiles too much
forgets everything

i command a flock of geese west of harrietsville to
change direction and fly over me they do up close i am
horrified every goose is flapping like crazy fly away i
command them and they do the princess of poems kisses
the earth

holding the opening of his new rubber boot up to his
ear thomas shouts from the back seat i can hear the
ocean

when i was nine i found out
my mother was an alien
marooned on earth with no hope of escape
this explained why her words
clawed their way to me so slowly
and her actions never reflected
the moment being lived
she was much farther away than any of us knew
once when i was looking for a dime
under the refrigerator i noticed
her feet didn't quite touch the ground
everything she did was a moment too soon
or a moment too late
she bandaged our fingers before we bled
wiped our tears before we cried

i have taken measures rearranged the whole downstairs
to make a place to work crammed my sons into the only
room with a door given them a couch chair tv vcr still
the typewriter sits cold papers lying around sometimes
i rush in stand looking down at the poems read one rush
out now i have a place to write

sitting in the car outside the arena since 6 it's noon
waiting for joel's game to be over thomas and james
burst in shouting and bringing in cold air excited
about something they're trying to tell me i'm writing
in my notebook they fight over who will tell me get out
i say they don't if you want to stay you'll have to be
quiet i reason they are for seven seconds they begin
again GET OUT i scream they jump out of the car and run
away the joy on their faces mystifies me

the dishwasher is leaking so bad the dog dish is
floating my socks get soaked when i answer the phone my
oldest son is calling to find out who said i think
therefore i am descartes i tell him ask me anything
after a pause he asks can i have a new pair of shoes
for the semi-formal

when i look up i don't see angels
i see fists
the stones in my driveway don't sing for me
i dream my ex-husband's throwing a tantrum
he can't keep what he's stolen
my blue woollen tights
a cashmere sweater

like marie d'oignies who buried bloody
mouthfuls of herself
in the garden
i need my poems to be like this

this room is cold it's all windows the fucking cat is
playing with something under my bed probably a dried
turd i'm ovulating dull pain in my little purse of eggs
james joyce's kids didn't go to hockey games or
bernardo's school of martial arts did he wash clothes
cook meals clean toilets

dreamed i was looking at my breasts in the mirror
noticed a strange circular shadow above my left nipple
upon closer inspection i discovered it was a third
nipple forming under the skin is this cancer i wondered

the trees are waiting
for the second coming
when christina miribilis floats up
to sit in their top branches
later she climbs down into a hot oven
full of bread
lies down between the baking loaves
watch me burn she screams
this is you in hell
afterwards she crawls out unharmed
looks for a high place to pray
where she won't smell
the living

here in the moment the forever

she wakes up before it's light
he's been awake all night again
watching for the police
he believes things that aren't true
he thinks because he took two cigarettes
from an acquaintance that the police are looking for him
the sons are upstairs
awake or sleeping
she's not sure

sometimes she wakes up and he's kneeling
beside the bed
tears running down his face
she offers to swallow him
but he jumps up and slams around in the closet
looking for suitcases
or runs outside in his socks
pretending to leave
but he comes back
the sons are upstairs
listening

then a breaking down before morning
the father downstairs
the sons upstairs
the minute hand falls into the refrigerator and breakfast
comes clattering across the lawn
its spoons and bowls and burning toast

she rests a while in the bed
remembering a warm barn
bins full of soybeans
lofts piled with hay
the caged ferret below
there it is   says the uncle
pointing through the wire and cobwebs

crossing fields of deep snow
the uncle and the father carry guns
she has the ferret
if she'd looked into the sky
instead of trying to plant her feet in
their big bootprints
she'd have seen her sons' faces
cloudy and expectant
watching her
we're coming someday
you can sing to us over and over
fill our bowls
the sweetest sweet
my babies
she might have thought
here in the moment the forever
my babies wait in a sky

the sons are coming down the stairs
into the 16th of september
the father is gone
fallen off the edge of circle ave
the mother and the sons are here
as if it were anywhere else and their faces
drift in and out of rooms
now and now and now
like the leaves falling into the pond years later
every leaf meeting its reflection
the sun burning white on the pond's face
the blue heron's nest deserted it's the way of the world
ducks so high and flying off
the spring phlox picked and pressed and sent away
in airmail envelopes

remember-me-here letters
the photographs
she sees the elderberries dried on the bush
her basket empty and elsewhere
don't   don't she says to nobody
adoring the sound of the reeds
most of all

mass strandings

this morning five-year-old thomas calls downstairs to me
there's worse things in the world than germs mom
what   i yell back
bears
what's the next worst thing i ask
after a moment he answers
gorillas
and what are the best things i ask
after a long silence
kittens and worms

later two young men are cleaning the living room furniture
for $39.99
mike with long greasy blonde hair is in charge
kyle's thin with brown hair and the beginnings of a moustache
early in the job mike exclaims
this is my favourite kind of couch to clean
why is that i ask and he tells me
because all the spots come off
he speaks with a passionate sincerity
you can tell this couch was scotch-guarded
scrubbing away at a dark stain on the arm
he stands up and steps back
arms out he looks as if he's about to embrace my couch
then a shadow of pain crosses his face
ma'am did you know that after a couch is cleaned the scotch-
guarding won't work?
for another $39.99 we'll scotch-guard it for you
okay i say reluctantly and go downstairs to fold laundry
embarrassed at being such an easy mark
while i match socks in the basement
i picture mike and kyle in my living room
grinning and winking and poking each other in the ribs
with their elbows

james who is seven sits on the stairs with thomas
he has decided to test his little brother
is a pet fish tamer than a wild fish
thomas stalls for time   ummm
yes or no demands james
no? thomas bravely supplies
wrong laughs james jumping up and running outside

dolphins often die in mass strandings i read they sometimes
follow the leader while feeding and are led to shallow water and
trapped or some mass strandings are the result of vicious storms
or they may be frightened by fishing boats or it could be
something to do with the earth's magnetic fields or pollution or
the exploding of depth charges by mining companies but it's never
on purpose says the article
strandings are divided into two categories
single and mass
lone dolphins become stranded because they are sick
mass strandings involve fifty or even a hundred dolphins at once
but it's definitely not suicide stresses the writer suicide
requires a high order of intelligence and is a willful act

it appears diligence is no guarantee against being stranded
it's topography in cahoots with coincidence
a depth charge alone is survivable
so is a divorce
so is cancer
but beware the gentle approach of the shoreline
the panic when you squirm
and your belly scrapes bottom

into the landscape

i am a teacher of young children
i have earned the right to speak of the heart
hundreds of children slip through my hands
their knees and elbows skinned daily
i hear them and hear them

christopher poked me in the eye
sarah pinched me
philip kicked me in my privates
courtney said a bad word to me
what was it i asked
liar
she said liar
jimmy said a bad word said andrew
what was it i asked
pissed said andrew pissed
pissed in my pants

i hear and the heart i wish to speak of
is the heart i help them hear and feel
here i tell them by the schoolyard fence
taste this
it's the edible end of a tender grass stem
it's the skin a little down and back of my lover's ear
it's justina's shiny black shoes with convertible straps
kari's jean jacket with brown plastic fringe

once i saw charlotte raven dawn's mother
outside the grocery store piling bags of groceries
into the back seat of a cox cab
her words launched like ships of convicts
hope torn off and spit out with her fingernails

every day bryan's mother waits for him
her body curved as an empty cup
fill me fill me
i watch from the big windows
hiding behind the butcher-paper rainbow

marshmallow birthday parties
days i can give them
the same the same the same
into the landscape of same the days of same
they walk and begin to learn

shoes

shut-up were my first words
her first words laughs my mother
and we had to wash her mouth out with soap
kiss my ass is what she yelled at my father
when he wasn't yelling it at her
and the five-finger word
flat and stinging hot on my cheek or on my
kiss my on my ass
or curled up
the size of anyone's heart

there are nineteen children in my class this year
but i won't remember them all
i will remember bradley and martha and ashley
martha for her tears
i never knew tears could be that big
and tracey who cried only once when she thought her
friend was going to break my wooden shoes
these are the most important shoes in the world to me
i told them
what does tracey know about my wooden shoes
the hollow noise they made in the hall

martha's father introduced himself
after the christmas concert
said several idiotic things before he reeled off
smelling of scotch
martha touches the boys' penises
with a chin-tucking smile like she's passing notes
reacts to pain with panic-stricken howls
and impossibly huge tears

bradley gets off the bus on the coldest morning in
february a shapeless bundle in snowsuit scarf hat boots
and runs out of the line of five-year-olds all of them
bundled up within an inch of their lives waving his
ninja turtle backpack yelling i've got something
important to tell you
get back in line bradley i say

is it fear
or the habit of fear
that brings teachers to this

it's a week before i remember the incident
and it's a painless recollection
a painless kiss my ass recollection
this morning bradley tries again
as i sit at the front of the 19 five- and six-year-olds
he comes to me
i have to tell you something important
and he leans into my right ear
cupping his hands to make a safe tunnel for his words
moist and warm
my grandpa has whispers growing out of his nose

last week ashley painted her paper red
edge to edge
then she added two pink windows
a pink door
a purple doorknob
she said it's valentine's day so my house is red
when my mom saw it she said   what happened
who's been painting our house
when my mom was sleeping my brother ate the windows
i ate the door and the doorknob and the bricks
and my mom said why is it so cold
how about we move over to daddy's house and i marry him
so we did

then i ate daddy's house
so we had to move to grandma's
her name is mel
i painted her house all red but i didn't eat it
i was too full

crammed onto the compulsory horse-drawn wagon taking
the compulsory ride through the compulsory apple
orchard ashley shows me the long white scar on her
forehead tells another story about how her mom got mad
and was pulling her through their house she on an
accident hit my head against the door and i went to the
hospital and got staples but i didn't tell my daddy
that i told my daddy i slipped because i was wearing my
clicky-clacky shoes the shiny black ones with the gold
bows but now i'm scared 'cause he always says ashley
get those shoes off and i love my clicky-clacky shoes

year

and fall of land for valleys tumble out
like inside nesting dolls the always creek

shiver and calls she winter spring green snow
sends quiver and shadow for play for eyes

budding slow her whisper and tender her
babies of scent of naked trees

for mouth her luscious summer for boots for
wet grass o sound of asking without or

desire or wondering without nor
hungry seasons of full pockets and notes

small of white of folded once or twice
of forget of known

notes

the letter poems in section two are based upon correspondence between elizabeth graves simcoe and mary anne burgess during the late 1700's when elizabeth was travelling in canada with her husband

the quotation from denise levertov comes from her statement for *The New American Poetry* in 1959 which i encountered in *Coming to Light: American Women Poets in the Twentieth Century*, edited by diane wood middlebrook and marilyn yalom

'suicide note for isis' remembers sylvia plath

tutuyea is an innu artist

christina miribilis and marie d'oignes were medieval christian visionaries

An ex-tobacco harvester, ex-psychiatric nurse's aid, and ex-market gardener, Julie Berry teaches kindergarten in her native St. Thomas, Ontario, where she lives with her four sons. She has been involved in the peace movement for years. Her poetry has appeared, or is forthcoming, in such journals as *Room of One's Own*, *Quarry*, and *Canadian Forum*. *worn thresholds* is her first book.